the shallow end of sleep

poems

José
Antonio
Rodríguez

TIA CHUCHA PRESS
LOS ANGELES

Printed in the United States of America

ISBN 978-1-882688-41-8

Book design: Jane Brunette
Cover photo: From the series Doorknobs and Cobwebs by Ryan G. Beckman.
Cover background photo: Hunter Reynolds
Back cover photo: Matthew Burns

PUBLISHED BY:

Tía Chucha Press
A Project of Tía Chucha's Centro Cultural, Inc.
PO Box 328
San Fernando, CA 91341
www.tiachucha.com

DISTRIBUTED BY:

Northwestern University Press
Chicago Distribution Center
11030 South Langley Avenue
Chicago, IL 60628

*Tía Chucha Press is the publishing wing of Tía Chucha's Centro Cultural, Inc., a
501 (c) 3 nonprofit corporation. Tía Chucha's Centro Cultural has received funding for
this book from the National Endowment for the Arts. Other funding for Tía Chucha's
Centro Cultural's programming and operations has come from the California Arts
Council, Los Angeles County Arts Commission, Los Angeles Department of Cultural
Affairs, The California Community Foundation, the Annenberg Foundation, Thrill
Hill Foundation, the Middleton Foundation, Not Just Us Foundation, the Weingart
Foundation, and others, as well as donations from Bruce Springsteen, John Densmore,
Lou Adler, Richard Foos, Adrienne Rich, Tom Hayden, Dave Marsh, Mel Gilman,
Jack Kornfield, Jesus Trevino, David Sandoval, Denise Chávez and John Randall of
the Border Book Festival, and Luis & Trini Rodríguez, among others.*

For the unkempt kid
in the classroom

contents

1

Piñatas Too Small for Candy / 6

Resident Alien Card / 11
Fuchsia / 13
Crushed Aspirin / 15
Between Snores and Polyester / 16
Like Waking Up All Over Again / 19
School Summer: Dimmit, Texas / 21
Kraft American Cheese / 23
Father / 25
Ghost Stories / 26
Giddy Gurgle / 27
Luis / 28
Doña Bruna / 29
Mud / 30
Ashes and Rocking Horse / 31

2

The Shallow End of Sleep / 35
Watching my father under the Chevy / 36
Avocado / 37
Playing Monopoly / 38
Geometry / 39
Freshman Class Schedule / 42
In a Yawn / 43
Joe, I never write about you / 44
Buick with Automatic Windows / 46
Violent Sky / 48
Whooping Cough (from my mother's memory) / 49
There Were Lizards / 50

3

Veins like Maps / 55
Fingerprints (dream of a woman who could've been my
mother as a young girl) / 57
The Glass Always Almost Invisible / 59
The Bean Plant in Kindergarten / 61
Blades of the Window Fan / 62
Posada / 63
Imagine a Tree / 64
The Confidence of Their Knees / 66
The missing is the point here, / 68
On watching a PBS documentary in the middle of the night / 69
Into the Dark Knots of Naked Walls / 72
Meaning Enough for Peaches / 74
The Little Rooms / 76

4

1979 Chicago Ave. / 81

Acknowledgments / 83

Piñatas Too Small for Candy

The only Mexicans in Binghamton
wait tables at the Mexican restaurant,
their accents thick and minimalist
as they take orders from twenty-year-olds
on cell-phones and iPods.

The walls around them
suspend stapled throw blankets –
one an image of an Aztec warrior
holding the limp body of a woman
against his bare chest,
his headdress oddly monochromatic;
another, the icon of the Virgin of Guadalupe,
head tilted, eyes downcast,
a poor replica of the altar
in the basilica.

Wal-Mart piñatas dangle
from the ceiling: donkeys and stars,
all sharp corners,
too small to hold any candy,
ribbons in random primary colors
bursting from them and flickering
around the icon of the Virgin.

The waiter's quick pencil stops
at the sound of my Spanish
without an accent, the sign
of some common foreignness
or exile,
while I wonder when my tongue
will trip on the trilled R's of my last name
now far from home where a wall
is being erected over the river
severing some limb
I never knew I had, its phantom
just beginning to throb.

Resident Alien Card

This is what I know
of that day: 5 years old
and being walked
through the immigrant process.
The photo first, two copies:
one for the eventual alien card
and one that gets lost in a cardboard box
without a label, until today.

The photographer has no face,
only a voice steady like the low light
from the corner of the studio,
the light that sometimes falls
on still bodies.
Look at the teddy bear on the wall.
It is faded, small and gray with dust
and dulled eyes, nailed to the wall,
a stab of rust through the belly.

I must turn my head to show
my right ear to the camera.
Right, not left, barks the voice
in the darkness. My tall mother stands
outside the lens trying to make herself small.

How ready was I to be clean in America,
shiny like a new quarter.
But the photo shows dark circles
under the eyes, hints of shadows.
I ask my mother while she scrubs dishes,
her hand soft around the rim,
and she says nothing, which is everything
because she doesn't say
      I don't see the circles.
      All children look that way.
      You're imagining things.

Though I remember that sleep
was hard to seduce in the shelters
of my childhood, this photo I run into
while visiting her for the summer –
all of 34 and well fed – this photo
burdens my hands with shame,
like stones I can't cast off.

Here is the evidence of lack –
exposed – obvious I know now
to the grownups at school,
to the mat of my kindergarten naps,
my body hugging the thin plastic foam.

Fuchsia

A brown curtain
with paisley drops of fuchsia
hangs between the one room
and the kitchen.

I lean close,
place my cracked lips
against the drops,
hoping to grow long limbs
from this cotton constellation.

My older sister
lays her bridesmaid dress
(on the bed), a red gown of soft
fabric that I hold tight like the roof
holds the walls of this dead house.

The fabric tears
because it is generous
and my sister yells words
that taste like raw potatoes
that I'm supposed to swallow.
To not do so would be cruel.
So this too is beauty.

I imagine the curtain,
how it must be tired
of hanging from a rope
nailed to the corners,
tired of pretending
to be a door because it must,
how it can't let itself be carried away.
The fibers teased by the dusty breeze
that lengthens my afternoons.

All night I smell the fuchsia
and hem the door frame
that expands so as not to touch the cotton
in the middle of a house without floor
or ceiling.

Not even the flies respect its borders
though the occasional butterfly does believe
the paisleys are flower petals.

My mother calls me to the table
to eat the twice refried beans
pushed against the rise of the plate,
opposite the absence of enamel –
a hole of rust shaped like a paisley drop
that is not fuchsia, not red.

Every piece of tortilla
must detach a morsel, sliding away
the part from the sum, feeding without waste.
Such dedication to the business of living.

I fling the plate out the open door
where the beans drop away
like mud off shoes. The plate
hits the ground, wobbles like an old tire.

A big spoon lands hard over my head
and I hear the enamel break,
though I don't bother turning
to see who it is, but run out
and throw myself on the ground,

sunlight washing over my eyelids,
making everything fuchsia,
or a red close enough to beautiful.

Crushed Aspirin

The cactus bush lunges back and forth
while I eat the potatoes
cooked in the dirt-filled barrel.
The thorns grow closer
with every tear from the tortilla.

The young chicken's eyes of earthbound lust,
its feathers dusty with desire,
betray the neck movements that aren't random.

My young old brother hits the chicken
with a stick. She gurgles something,
drags herself under the cactus.
I keep eating the half raw mush.

Birds know nothing of empty butane gas tanks.
They know of mulberry-bush branches,
of lesser classes, the flightless ones.

The pruned corn kernels could be viruses.

The aspirin crushed in a cup of water
doesn't bring her back from the heavy lidded stare
of the noonday wrinkled air
though she drinks like a feverish patient.

Though I am the youngest, I know
walking in crooked lines gets you lost
in the backyard cemetery,
where single-lane roads dead end
into mesquite trunks, rotted.

Mother makes chicken soup,
a small bowl of metal soot.
I close my eyes and spoon it all.

Between Snores and Polyester

I know to climb on the bed
before you start spreading out blankets
on the floor for my sisters.

I've heard them complain that I wet myself
and that this eventually wakes them.

This is the solution.
By the time you climb in,
dad is already snoring.
I tell you about school,
how cool that place, how odd
that the classroom is never warm
and how I can't seem to get used to it.

You mutter a few syllables
and finally turn over on your left side,
your back to me.

Dad behind me is safe against the one window.
Your nightgown feels slippery
like a nylon or plastic bag.
Polyester, you keep saying.

I ask you again why you have to turn away
and again you say nothing.

The moon light trickles
through the screen door, gray
and I imagine cool but it falls
only on the bodies of my sisters.

Before I no longer know if I'm awake,
my eyes smell the sweat beneath me,
the pillow damp
the blanket at my ankles –

ruffles like the wind-beaten
paper flowers for the dead.
I imagine sleeping face up for once,
arm-and-leg-out like the kids
in Saturday morning TV commercials,
and I try but dad's shoulder digs into my spine.

I imagine inhaling moon light

and urine and dad's snores.
I imagine the walls of the room expanding,
the roof collapsing
the rats crawling around my hair,
their fur oily too because they mustn't bathe
but I wouldn't mind.

Your head leans out too far
and bumps against the chest of drawers,
the one my aunt gave us
because she had a new one.
Beyond it is a cot, then a wall.
This is the tight order.
You begin to weep, quietly
and I know to pretend not to hear.

I feel bad that mice must wait until night-time
to look for food. Wouldn't mind sharing
the table with them because they wouldn't
take up much space.
They could use my sister's toy tea set –
        just the right size.

You stop weeping.

I move one inch closer
while my lungs lean against my ribs
and I must remember to breathe shallow
like the irrigation ditch of my father's crops.
These are the prayers I hum,
the prayers I don't yet know the words to.

Tomorrow morning my underwear will be stained
but tonight I wrap my free arm over your belly,
which is soft and warm
and I whisper *If your body leans too far
beyond the mattress, I will hold you.*
Then I chuckle because I am small
and you are heavy. Then I sleep, yes
but never fall.

Like Waking Up All Over Again

A soft voice that hints at a slow-burning panic wakes me,
nudges my shoulder until I move into a night
made a little less lonely by the light from a lamp post

that seeps in through the window high in the wall
like an eye or an altar - it caresses the floor boards,
the blankets ruffled and recently bereft of our bodies.

The stove, table and refrigerator remain motionless
up against the opposite wall like a police lineup.
A pair of arms lifts me and I move out and outside

into a morning mist that reminds me of the ooze of crushed insects.
Pairs of arms and legs climb the bed of a pickup truck,
the grass up to my knees. I can still see stars.

The doors open, mangled metal like a monster
uttering something in anger. The dirt and drool mix to form mud.
I follow, jump off onto the road that outlines the onion fields.

The foreman tells the families you have to finish picking one row
before starting another. His voice is a fox in a receding darkness,

the orange sun always revealing and outlining the limits of our summers,
the brittle walls of the barracks, the aluminum beer cans in dumpsters,
the icy water from a hose lapping my back at the end of the day.

The rows fade into each other, rush toward the sloping horizon.
The lack of markers - trees, street blocks, signs - unsettles me,
like waking up all over again. I am terrified.

Everybody bends at the waist because kneeling wastes time.
I tell myself that I must learn the backs of my parents,
memorize the line of their vertebrae, the curve of their haunches,

the glean of their napes under the sun in all its stations
so that I don't lose them in the dirt rows that run away from me
into the distant sky, teeming with onions – all these heads limbless

and swiftly chopped with metal shears. After a few hours I raise my head,
turn my eyes to the portable toilets, bright turquoise boxes,
beautiful, a balm for my irises heavy with the color of tilled earth.

School Summer: Dimmit, Texas

Nose bleeds
that I can taste,
back-wash down
thick like overused car oil,
lean snot that turns brown
dull,
not like the sun
that lays its unfortunate
gifts on the body.

Pinch the nostrils,
breathe mouth open wide,
swallow
head back.
Catch a glimpse
of television -
in color!
Mom on a small stool,
arms folded
into themselves.

I retch though I'm empty.

Clean clinic doctors
float around me
in white tunics
that could never be soiled
by my body covered
in the summer dust
of the onion field.

Is it wrong to want to stay?

The baritone waves wash
over my bloody chest:
Let us take care of this. Lie back.

      Whatever you say.

Kraft American Cheese

This pale orange thing
is on the Frito pie,
on the sandwich commercials,
even on the enchiladas
at the school cafeteria.
Melted, gooey or sliced is all the same.

The commercial calls it Kraft American cheese,
the melody like a line of marching soldiers.
I place it between
two pieces of bread softer than any mattress,
whiter than any school wall,
so abundant in the grocery stores –
buildings larger than my dreams.
No bologna, no lettuce,
not even the tomato I love,
because I might vomit
and waste more food.

The aroma of this cheese
gives me a headache
but I want to love it
the way the boy in the television
loves it, the way the kids at school
swallow it without chewing.
Easy like the English language
sliding from their tongues,
their compartmentalized plates
soon scraped clean
but for the beans and rice
destined to become garbage.

My mother would turn away from this sight.
I've learned not to.

I take small bites
so I can breathe through my mouth
as I chew. The stairs creak
under my weight
as I sit outside the kitchen door,
hope that the scent of the bougainvillea,
the one my mother planted by the fence,
will perfume this American cheese
into something I can learn to swallow.

Father

He is arrived covered in dust
as if draped in a mosquito net,
         with beige eyelashes
from the citrus orchards.
He makes his way to the bathroom
in small steps –
         Toe heel toe heel toe heel.

The running water is a church choir
in the background of my games.
         I am always the geisha
in a play-pretend without geishas.

He sits under the porch
in weathered khakis
always khakis –
         a photograph I never took –
and a white crewneck
with a small tear at the stitch of his left armpit.
He stretches and I glimpse pale skin,
like the cheek of a neighbor's baby.
His shirted chest reminds me of a pillow,
         one that would never end
         flat and hard with drool.
Dame un piquito, he requests, as he leans.
And I kiss him on the lips, a peck
with curious traces of Brute
and a stiff moustache that pricks me.
It hurts and I smile still.

Ghost Stories

The teacher, all manicured white hands,
plays a ghost story on a record player
because Halloween is almost here.

The class is only three students,
and the other two boys,
like little piles of clothes
on a soft couch, tell her I carry
my books like a girl. I chuckle
because I do, the cricket chirping
in the corner of the room tells me so.

They chuckle back because laughter is
that way – contagious. Then
that I talk like a girl, their mocking
like costume jewelry I hold in the hollow
of my mouth. I smile lips-together
and my jaw doesn't ache.

Then about names flung, about
how others snatch my books,
tear away the golden covers,
Wonderbread ads scattered
across the asphalt of the basketball court,
every loose pebble warm in my hand.

Then they get up as if leaving,
small bodies and hunched backs
sheathed in t-shirts thin from overuse,
books straining their bony wrists.
Then the ghost story ends and nobody speaks.

Giddy Gurgle

Mother liked them, a bleeding man
with drops of red that never dried
and dulled to brown.

The house now almost possessed,
gloomy with the weight
of the crosses.

Some were portraits with eyes
that wept like the leading men
of telenovelas. Some were sculptures:

ivory, bronze, shivering metal.
Less red on those so the body
would compensate: the arch of the back

like a hook, the legs desiccated
like chicken bones, the face
a cartoon imitation of a prophet.

But one day the dilated wells of my eyes
crawled south and found Him
and only a sliver of cotton.

That night when I shut
the knob-less door to pray,
I saw him born in the black hole

of a ceiling star, coming down
off the cross and gripping me tight.
Held in the baptism of moans,

the giddy gurgle of my filthy dreams
smoldering under my mole-pocked skin.

Luis

His riverbank eyes rippled
when he'd tell me stories
of his older brothers' neighborhood fights,
when I'd tell him of my time spent
in the library searching for pop-up books
I heard of but could never find.
Feeding our skinny bodies on dreams.

How many friends you got besides me?
he'd ask on the way home, all dimples and freckles
on his milky quartz face that I wanted to touch.
And I never knew how to answer.

Breathe through your nose,
our mothers warned us before
winter morning walks to take the school bus,
believing we might keep out the world's ills
by keeping our mouths sealed.

Luis merely grinned then, his lips
tight against each other. There was little to say
those times when every word was a risk.

But one blue morning out on the curb,
the sharp wind flaying our hands
wrapped around our books,
he moved to stand between me and the wind
and said *We'll take turns.*

So I did it, opened my lips and answered him
You, Luis, just you.

And his smile grew until I saw his teeth.

Doña Bruna

Doña Bruna, the witch,
welcomes the child
onto handmade polyester
quilts and rock slab pillows,
spreads his nervous arms
in the form of a cross,
smiles at his eyes brilliant
like flies in a lidless jar.

Doña Bruna renders sounds
from her books without letters.

Puede ser mal-de-ojo.[1]

Here, outside her home,
husbands have planted seeds of corn
have felt the weight of fathers fall on them
have then touched the misty fields. Here,
the fatigue of old wood ends old men's hearts.
Rows of corn open to become caskets.
Spirits hide in father's beds, stay for weeks
while bodies rock themselves into fetuses
and stare at the ants that stop for no one.

Today the boy closes his eyes
under the odorless herbs
          that sweep across his face.

[1] Spanish for *Could be the evil-eye*

Mud

under my huaraches[1]
on the rim of these
huaraches
that use to be
almost pretty.
My house drowns
every time the rain pecks
at the flea market leather
of my huaraches.
My wrinkled toes cramp.
On the step – one lip
that blows half kisses
to the overflowing canal water,
on the door frame
of this wet still-life,
on the wrinkled forearm
of my dead grandfather,
on the ground that swallows
the foot of the bed
is mud,
grainy with the crushed glass
of windshields from one-car accidents,
brown and boiling cold
with earthworms that squirm
under the bed sheet,
insinuate themselves,
curious but blind.

[1] Spanish for *sandals*

Ashes and Rocking Horse

The garbage heap simmered,
the last of the neighbor's
unwanted things smoking
then only like the tail end
of my father's cigarette,

while I sifted
for a coffee cup without a handle
a pair of toy car tires
that made me believe myself
lucky when something crafted
survived the burning.

The ash felt tender between
my toes, clang to my feet,
flitted up my calves
marked by the detritus
of a world once on fire.
Shapes like ancient maps.

One day the neighbor's line
of elegant pines swayed apart
to reveal a rocking horse on their patio –
painted in the colors of the cake
at the bakery, the one behind glass.

The soles of my feet knew
to be cautious, only toes and heel,
to avoid nails or cut glass.
Smoke always a warning.

For weeks, I came to bathe
in the gray breeze and stare at the horse
that made the wind sing beautiful
when it moved inside it.

Only glances really
like the one at the cake, like the one
at the smoldering plastic melting
into something unrecognizable.
Then the horse was not there
and the only thing among the ashes
was a doll's head
with one eye burned away.

2

The Shallow End of Sleep

Some nights whole seasons
settled inside me. Some nights

I couldn't breathe. Some nights
I woke, skin damp under salty sheets.

I knew nothing of oceans.

Some nights I stepped outside
where moon light made my arms ashen.

My legs looked foreign
but my pee would gurgle

in the trampled grass and splash
my calves. A horse tied to a pole

would watch me through black eye sockets
and long eyelashes like slivers of nightclouds.

I'd scurry back behind the screen door
with mangled wire mesh that scratched

at my left hand. And the bed
was a small body of water

and no matter how hard I tried to slip away,
the shore was always visible.

Watching my father under the Chevy

The old man, bent over the motor
his back like the bricks
of his unfinished home
listens for a hum,
senses with hands
that need another coat of Vaseline
for aluminum shivers —
one-eyed spark plugs
and hoses congested
with the nests of dirt road moths.

The upper lip sweats
the small work of fingertips
while the eyelids squint
and murmur bluff bargains
to a smooth-faced god.

When he sees it,
he straightens his knotted back,
      pulls out from his wrinkled pocket
      a damp handkerchief
      wipes his brow
and nods –
      Well, now I know.

Avocado

My crotch feels warm before I know to hold it in.
The wet blankets will soon be colder than they were last night.

The snores of those who sleep are muffled by heavy fabric.
I get out of bed and I don't mind the jeans and jacket so much anymore,

how denim clings to bed sheets, how nylon slides away.
I'm hungry and the aroma of the avocado makes me almost myopic.

This morning, though, the avocado is harder than I remembered it.
Spoons are always dull. The cold of the kitchen walls pulls at my skin

so that I feel like the tips of my fingers are coming undone.
The knuckles tighten and I think of my youngish aunt who moves

with a cane. Maybe the body dies not all at once but in pieces.
The tortilla for the avocado taco blackens over the stove burner

but my fingers don't burn when I touch the part that smolders.
I place my hands close to the flame — blue with an orange center —

and soon the scent of burnt hair, fine like ice crystals, fills the space
before me. I no longer think of the avocado exposed, blackening.

My hands ache something new like my next birthday, but I don't cry
and I wish my father could see me. Later that morning

the TV will mention an overnight freeze, damage to the citrus orchards
my father tended to in the night. Within a year he will be out of work,

will leave far in search of orchards green instead of ice burnt.
I'll promise to him that I will no longer wet my bed. I won't cry.

Instead, I will hand him an avocado and tell him to cut it open
　　on a warm day.

Playing Monopoly

Eleven dollars but worth it all
because we could share it.
And when my sister, who'd first seen it for real
at the Boy's Club where she worked,
held the box in her hands, it shimmered
bright and un-dented, like everything
I thought I wanted my life to be.

The Saturday morning TV commercial promised
joy accruing wealth like the jingle of coins
in a piggy bank, investing in properties and hoping
people couldn't afford them – the green homes
with perfect corners, the red hotels
that looked like the textbook picture
of George Washington's home. The kids gloated
guiltless when they won and the losers frowned
for a second, their hands empty,
until they all decided to play again,
like losing and winning were nothing.

We read the rules in our new English,
laid out the cards of Chance, Community Chest –
pretending we knew what a large word
like community meant – thumbed the money,
the smooth bills that gave themselves easily to dreaming.
When one of us landed on Park Place,
we chuckled nervously. Nobody bought it.

When I beat my brother in the end,
he smiled at the nothing between his hands.

We all laid the paper money back in the pockets,
astronomical sums, metal miniatures,
cards secured by rubber bands,
plastic homes in little bags.

I could tell you that I thought then of everybody
putting in late hours, pooling money together
to eke out the $400 payment on the house
with a sink that drained into a bucket,
with curtains for doors, with broken mattresses
for beds, but it wasn't like that –
thoughts lined neatly like blocks.

It was like when you finished your serving of beans
and knew not to ask for seconds,
that moment between taking the last bite
and pulling the chair away from the table,
the taste of that and the swallowing.

Geometry

His black mane undulates
in harmony with the muscles
intimate to the arms that finish digging
what will be an old-man's grave.

My uncle is dead
and the man digging is my brother.

A long-dead aunt's remains lie mute
in one corner of the grave,
in a black garbage bag -
>bones that architect this cemetery
>of giant crowns, hard paper flowers.
>The styrofoam wreaths are no longer white
>but beige, brown really.

He throws the shovel out.
The mourners divide by gender.
I lean toward the women
and the men eye my careful distance.

My brother lifts the bag
for someone to take to lighten his ascent
to the world of things with names.
The dead man's daughter weeps,
the other women pray while standing
and the men walk around moving dirt.

I take the bag.
I take the bag to calculate
the heavy,
to feel the geometry –
wooden toy blocks
that spell something simple.

The remnants of femur and tibia jostle,
moved by the music of loosening petals
and the murmur of mourners'
long skirts and sleeves held down
with hands and deliberate buttons.

My arm strains
angular and skinny
but the tissue covers everything.

And hair decays more slowly than tissue.
And the eyelashes must have been the last to go.

Freshman Class Schedule

I hate my freshman class schedule.
I'm in Algebra I, an advanced class
but not the most advanced,
which is where my friends are.

I'm stuck with idiots who don't understand
the relationships of angles.
It's all in the triangle, I want to scream
beneath my too-easy smile.

After the graduation ceremony,
my friends will walk away forever,
become engineers with expensive shoes,
sensibly-sized families. Even now
they're getting whiter every day.
Dreams of albino dollar bills
coat their pillows, I know it,

while I grow brown.
Brown like my father's forearms
which my freckle-faced mother insists
are only brown because of the years
bent over fields Brown like the custodians
Brown like the Dairy Queen workers
Brown like the drop-outs
Brown like the juvies
Brown like the machos
Brown like the earthen floor
Brown like the outhouse
Brown like the soles of my feet when I run.

In a Yawn

When I was five
I dreamt of saddling
the only pig in the pen –
        a tumble weed
        of copper wire hair
        on skinny legs
        like those of my oldest uncle
        who I heard drank too much
        and neglected his kids –
and riding it to the end of the dirt road.

The pebbles would bounce off
the pale hooves and brush my cheeks,
but I'd only wipe the sweat off my face,
ignore the pebbles.
I could reach the other end
of the cornfield before nighttime
and we could sleep together,
me resting on its warm belly.

The moon is not made of cheese
and never looked like it.
Still I'd swallow it,
breathe it in through my mouth
before closing my eyes.

But pigs can't be saddled
and my father sold the last horse
for a pick-up truck without a windshield.

Joe, I never write about you.

When I write about friends, I write
about Luis from kindergarten,
about how he grew up to be a gangbanger,
how I think he dropped out of school,
how I don't know because even though
I befriended his brother in college,
I never asked about him.

Or I write about my friends from 6th grade
because I still keep in touch because
they live in Austin and drive nice cars
but still keep it real.

But I never write about Joe,
my friend from 5th grade. I never write
about how his mother fed me
buttered toast because breakfast at home
was sometimes not enough, how
I never told my mother
that I wasn't being a polite boy
and refusing food, how
we did all our homework together, how
he lived one block down
in a two-room shack
       smaller even than my family's
how he was the first one to get my jokes,
how he laughed, sometimes
at nothing in particular. How one day
my sister and I were leaning on the fence
      in front of our house
      swatting away flies.

How Joe walked by
on the other side of the street,
how his jeans were tight, how
they were too short for him.

How before I could wave hi to Joe
my sister called him a faggot
because of the way he walked
          hips swishing, head bobbing.

How she didn't say it to him
but whispered it to me. How
at that moment
the late afternoon sky suddenly dimmed,
just a little. How only I noticed.

No, I never write about how
I never spoke to him after that day. How
I moved on to 6th grade,
to a gifted-and-talented program in a new school
while he moved on to 6th grade,
to a not-gifted-and-talented program in the old school.

How we couldn't be friends anymore
because we were now in different schools. How
he lived down the block.

Buick with Automatic Windows

My father has driven
for twelve hours up the Texas flatlands.
The sun is setting, like walking away.
I am fourteen and sit
in the backseat with my sister.

We've come up through the pan handle
to find work around the town of Dimmit
during the summer break,
stoop labor of some kind,
and I don't look forward
to the early morning dew that soaks
muddy shoes and canvas gloves.

I say nothing. We pull over,
park by a gas station
and sleep in the Buick that has roared
windows-down all day.
The few words uttered fade
into the cracks of the dashboard
and my family is soon snoring.

First I try sitting upright,
my head against the velveteen headrest.
Then I try bending at the waist,
letting my torso rest on the seat,
the nape of my neck tight
against my sister's thigh. Finally,
my body slumps on the floor,
my head and shoulders on the lip
of the seat, the softest part,
but nothing works.

The night cools but not enough
to warrant windows nearly shut.
Just two inches of air
up near the ceiling.

My hand reaches for the button
to lower the window
but it doesn't work, I discover.

I'd thought this new used Buick fancy
because it had automatic windows,
a first for us. I ignored
the cigarette-burned seats,
the sun-warped plastic armrests.
No more muscle work to turn a crank,
just one finger. The effort hardly noticeable.

But here, crouched in the pit of night
I'm trapped in this supposed thing of luxury.

I won't wake my father to insert the key,
nor will I open the door – wake everyone –
to the foreign world of blue-eyed people.

So I sit back up, glance out
at the light posts over the gas pumps
so white they obscure the stars
straining behind them.

Violent Sky

The hurricane winds take away the light.
We place lit matches against candle wicks
and wait for the storm to amble away,
hoping for dust through a screen door.

Water trickles in through the stove exhaust,
streams down the wall behind the stove
of this new house built by my sister's office job,
concrete floor, brick walls, and a roof
that is not also a ceiling.

When my mother sees the trickle,
she sighs and reaches for a kitchen towel.

Water has followed me to every dry place,
she whispers, lips tight,
eyes brilliant with the coming tears
that she tries to swallow.

I tell her the roof will be fixed,
that not even our feet will touch water,
but she keeps wringing her hands.

I do the math of years in brittle rooms
that inevitably succumbed to rains and floods
like paper boats, and the answer startles me
so that I stand up, walk to the window.

This science in my head can't shelter her,
can't smooth the places inside that will never dry –
living life like treading water.

She moves to the couch, the towel in her lap.
Her silhouette is still by the candle light
that flickers faithfully over the end table,
her eyes focused on the bars of the window,
the world outside beaten by a violent sky.

Whooping Cough (from my mother's memory)

The limbs flounder.
The sounds inhuman, coarse
jagged gusts that cut
through old sewer tunnels.

I hold her torso away
arms out
so she can see me.
But her eyes are marbles.

Then she goes limp
like wet cotton sheets.
Her mouth grey
exhausted
with the scent of ash trees.
Faint lavender sweet.

Ay güera, ni pa' qué, se te va a morir.[1]
    The flames of the fire pit crack my lips.
    This morning, while she slept over swept mud,
    I made sure the jars of sugar and coffee were
    sealed tight.
    Distant fat clouds call out the ants.
    The shelves are so flimsy.
The words of my comadre spill and mingle
with my baby's spittle that I wipe from her rotting peach lips
with my pink hand.
And I lick but it is tasteless
like a Sunday Eucharist.

The coffee pot totters over the fire
that threatens to escape from the pit.
The oxygen molecules hold on
greedily
    to the walls inside.

[1] Spanish for *Nothing to do, honey, she's gonna die on you.*

There Were Lizards

Goats kiss my fingers.
Chickens scratch at my toes.
The path to the door is overgrown
with nameless weeds.

My aunt has strung a fence
around my childhood home
now a shelter for animals
she will slaughter or sell.

The roof rusts. The floor is
pocked with goat shit. Holes of rot
through the walls let in light.

I wait for nighttime to come
and undress like I did on rainy days
when I was five.
The goats begin to chew my clothes.

I want to believe that windows remember
the wind of better years, that doors
hold traces of moonlight cobwebs.

I walk to the corner
of what was the kitchen
            because the mud-caked walls
            still hold the branches here.
Then close my eyes to the ceiling spiders
and forget that there was once an outhouse
ten steps away that made me fear the dark
of falling through.

In the corner I crouch
so that my testicles don't hang
            but are cradled
like bird's eggs in a nest.

There were lizards   many
that ran through the kitchen,
in one door, out the other.

But sometimes they'd stop,
sometimes they'd stare –
I under the kitchen table
banging the earthen floor
with swelling hands.

Here, within the crumbling
of makeshift fences, I scrape
my temple against the wall
and bleed frayed memories.

3

Veins like Maps

My mother limps.
I shouldn't have had
so many children, she says.
I am twelve. It is easier
to remember her words in English,
once removed from her
memories in Spanish.
But your father didn't believe
in contraception. To him,
women who took them were whores.

I say thank you a hundred times,
       whisper it to her
when she sleeps in the afternoons,
though I'm not sure why.

I sit carefully on the couch
that is thin foam and hard boards.
It is always too hot to be indoors,
           too hot to sleep.

I am four years old and I am old.
This heat ages everything it touches.
     My mother fans my face
with my one checkered shirt
beside the moonlight
that seeps onto the bed
where too many of us sleep
in wet cocoons. I know she has fallen
asleep because I grow hot.
So I wake her.

She fans me
despite the daily back and forth
to spoon water from the well.
Despite the slow beans over the fire pit.
Despite the outhouse that creeks,
that hides spiders and lizards
that stare and never become familiar.

I walk back to the kitchen
where she stands half-awake
boiling beans for dinner.

I can't undo all that has distended
        your veins that are maps
        leading to the past –
        distant because the curves
        on the dirt road obscure it
        and near because it still bleeds.
This I try to say with my eyes,
my irises the color of dust that coats everything.

Fingerprints (dream of a woman who could've been my mother as a young girl)

She didn't know that she loved being young.
Like the morning before a storm.
Then life was a pregnant dream
        still but quivering awkward
        like crab legs on a crab.
She had a name
though it will not be called forth.
The other never-sent postcard girls
in braids and pale suntans called her
down to the river
        fearless in its deep womb.

When the dream quivered into feverish motion
she knew that her hands could burden the weight
of an old screen door, even if they could not open it
behind the screams and yells she never uttered.
Her bare feet could feel the mineral of the earth in the shade.

Despite the absence, they started eroding,
burying themselves under the weight
of blind fetuses with nearsighted slits for eyes,
        all of them fooled into existence
        like afterbirth without birth
        under the suds of cheap detergent
        like wire mesh twisting in soiled cloth diapers
        cringing the wound from the fire pit,
        mute before the pricks of so many thorns
        from the cactus eventually edible.

One Sunday she felt her hands smooth
as a host without its Eucharist. She would imagine
a hill disappearing into the plains,
but there have never been hills here.

And if she was not her first-born scars
she was the names that clung to her
like dust to window frames,
             the echoes of *amá* and *mujer*
like the mermaid from the lotería
singing a song to herself.

And the quilts of thick polyester patches
never meant for walls
were no longer jaundiced yellow,
but dark like the water well, a shapeless weight
around her hands with faceless fingers,
only traces of where a mouth and eyes used to be.

And the streams charging toward the distant whole,
beyond cracked cornfields and checkpoint borders,
held behind the dam like curtained windows,
until her mind could dream her hands
into freshly turned soil settling into the rows
and pulling away light with iron magnetized
by the pulse of an undulating body in a river.

The Glass Always Almost Invisible

Something about a holiday break
sits in the back of my mind
in a Houston airport.

The connecting flight is running late,
a screen matrix of numbers and cities
listing a time delay of one hour.

But I am patient; there is so much
to entertain me.

I window shop watches and books,
then stand in line to order a slice of pizza
and a Coke.

People move around like plastic flakes
in a snow globe – hushed.

So very cosmopolitan, I think

and smile between morsels of pizza
because this is America and I am in it –
the airport walls lacquered white,
the large glass windows almost walls,
always almost invisible.

I feel successful when I fly –
the ticket in my back pocket a prize
I got for being a good boy,
for being the best boy, for learning to love
the smell of the linoleum floor
every morning, for raising my hand
every time, for staying out of playground fights.

When I return to the terminal,
the screen simply reads *Delayed.*

There is crowding of bodies –
this terminal a cul-de-sac
pregnant with frustrated plans.

All the seats are occupied
and more people keep coming –
their shoulders slump before the screen
and almost genuflect
as they place their luggage on the floor.

They walk away using polite tones –
"Excuse me."
"Sorry"
"Would you mind moving over?" –
as they make a space along the wall
and slump to the floor.

Windows grow dark behind my shoulders.
People begin spreading out coats,
anything of bulk that could become a bed
or a pillow.
They must learn to love
the smell of the thin carpet.

I walk away – the stink of too many bodies
choking me, my duffel bag banging against my calf –
and return to the store that sells watches.
Fossil it says in small metallic letters
on every face.
I lean my head against the display window,
all the faces brilliant under tiny light bulbs
placed just so to flatter them,
the glass always almost invisible.

The Bean Plant in Kindergarten

We made jack o' lantern cut-outs
from orange construction paper.
The table was level, smooth.
I imagined dragging it home,

my family sitting around it playing bingo
instead of pressing elbows
against the peeling floor,
all of it slanted, making sure
the beans we used to mark our sheets
didn't roll away but were returned
to the sack to be consumed.

The teacher, dressed in fabric the color
of the last birthday boy's gingerbread cake,
leaned over my left shoulder
and smiled at the even segments.

Along the windowsills behind me,
bean plants pushed through dirt
inside pint-sized milk cartons, their
little vines crawling toward light.

Look how they lean on the glass
the teacher cooed every afternoon.

Eventually the leaves would begin to shrivel
and then no amount of water would save them.

Blades of the Window Fan

The grill is an amputation
of an old box spring
that supports the pot of beans
which are young sediment
and the bed, knowing of its wholeness,
commits to the memory of pink walls
the steady weight, the soft curve of elbow
before the necessity of slow dismemberment
and loss.

I lie on a bed of weathered sheets
       dank and lined with the old maps of explorers
       trampled on by my father's small horse.
The coils below squeak out rusty crow feathers
to flame the fires in the pit outside.

The blades of the window fan
hypnotize my dirt brown stare,
dry away the sweat and urine
of wind-laced days without baths
in a bucket of well water.

Outside the window
the neighbor's dog surrenders
under the low mesquite branch
in a shallow hole it has dug
and lined with feathers – black
with blue and violet reflections
like the eye of a horse.

The rhythmic hum weighs down the eyelids
and kindles the fire.

The beans begin to boil.

Posada[1]

The older children
who know to bathe
before strutting along the railroad tracks
with clean wet hair like tar,
zip, button and buckle.

The young ones
remember the bags of candy
given out at the one-room church
at last year's posada,
and ask for one tonight.

Everybody wants the cookies and peanuts
that commemorate the birth of el niño Dios.
Hard candy rains down on him
even though he is toothless.

They wait indoors while the virgin gives birth
for the last time behind the house
then holds the baby close.

She leaves for many years to tend
to sorghum fields and mothered orphans.
When she is wrinkled and concave,
she returns to her son
so he may suckle on her breasts
that hang like old socks. The milk
is spoiled like the church mass prayers.

Nobody knows this is the last posada.
Everybody smiles over thin candles
while the chilly night dangles
from the tin roof like black snow.

[1]Christmas festivity centered around the nativity-scene theme

Imagine a Tree

a mesquite
about thirty feet tall,
leans away from the house
somebody's house
I never spoke to the owners
or their children.
Leans over the street.

Imagine two children,
walk home
the tree selfish between them
and the weakened light of young evening sun
now pleasurable.
Imagine one child carries a bag of groceries,
nothing special
eggs, potatoes, a gallon of milk.
The house is getting closer
tumbling into their eyes
like a seduction.
Their mother waits for a rescue.
Both hope she won't be weeping
on the couch,
which means no warm dinner,
which means animal cookies and Kool-Aid.
The boy says it's my turn to carry the bag
but the girl won't let it go.

Imagine a girl silent.
Imagine spite.
Imagine a boy spanked
for wearing a skirt.
Imagine random beads of sweat
over their bodies,
over days, maybe years
seeping back into their organs

their hearts soaked.
Imagine tired muscle.

The boy tickles the girl so she will
give up the bag.
She cries.
He tickles.
She doesn't.
Imagine entering the house,
one room with two beds and a stove,
a flimsy curtain dangling between
and no doors to slam shut.

The Confidence of Their Knees

They didn't only know
that one word, the guys
from my old high school hallways.
They knew other words, yes,
other words besides faggot.

When they weren't looking,
I'd watch them move their lips
pink and delicate. I see them still,
waiting for the bus after school.

The confidence of their knees,
a 45 degree angle between them,
their hands resting on their laps,
fingers curved over their crotches.
How they wear their cowboy shirts
tight under leather belts
and unbuttoned midway down
their torsos, three buttons I think.
Yes, three.

And their smooth dark chests
breathe out sweet words
to their girlfriends, who parade
before them in short denim skirts
and red lipstick, move around them
like this is their bedroom,
like this is midnight,
not four in the afternoon.
Their laughter betrays
the boys they still are.

But weren't they hard pillars
of menace in those snake skin boots
with sharp edges bought
in the shops of Mexico? How they
moved like wild cats, muscles
smooth with gravity under tight jeans.
The yellow transport inadequate
for their skin with its thin layer
of perspiration. How it shimmered
                              under the sun.

Yes, they knew other words,
words that made women smile,
that made their friends wink
– eyes flickering in complicity –
like they were inside something
like magic, something I suspected
I would never find in my books.

They are gone now,
and my hairline recedes faster
than I can run. And if I have to see them,
those boys, now managing a McDonald's
or getting an advance on their income tax
or making arrests in their old neighborhoods,
I'd rather close my eyes, see them
skip the bus the way they sometimes did,
and walk away into the sun.

The missing is the point here,

what I'm trying to say.
Returning every day
to the last murmur of the fire,
lifting every broken thing
missing a part.

Tell me if these things
make us whole,
make us the sum
of what we've seen and touched.

Because aren't we
this constant piecing
together – the toy block
with a letter, every morning
hands raking for one more letter:

Here the charred corners,
here the scraped edges
where there was color once.
Touch how it comes back –
distilled. This thing rescued.
This thing of beauty.

On watching a PBS documentary
in the middle of the night

1
The woman speaks
to someone just left
of the camera,
speaks Spanish.

Her tongue the only thing
that strikes me
amid the evening ills
of this black aquarium.

In a maquiladora
along the far side of the border
she assembles and sterilizes,
with the acidity of her tired breath,
the things that could
become my paycheck.

Her apron, color-coded
to distinguish rank, to situate,
dangles from a wire hanger
in the background of a window,
while in the foreground
she exhales the names of *patrones* –
>Panasonic
>Sanyo
>Memorex
in a coached deliverance.

They don't let her just talk.

2

In the desert, lizards
the color of bark have seen things
like strands of brown hair
around the branches of the huisache.

A poet from a South American country
composes poems about the dead women.

According to the interview of a journalist,
the gown for the quinceañera
in Ciudad Juárez
hangs in anxious corners
                    closets without walls
because the 14 year-old never returned.

Lollipops prepare girls for long hair
and doll dreams of a different kind.

The carnival never makes a stop
because the money for the party
was spent on the coffin
that holds parched bones   scattered teeth.

Even the plants of the desert
sport fangs that pierce fabric
with eyelets only
because the buttons are gone   torn off.

The hurried stitches of machines
never give as easily
as those of hand-knit scarves.

Caffeine keeps the arms in motion
for 16-hour shifts and makes tremors
almost an affliction.

The sands are never glamorous.

3

The woman speaks to someone
who listens with her eyes,
recalls a biblical battle
between a giant and a small man
with a bilingual name,
while she washes clothes
in a stream the color of steel.

But still – a man.

We want to forget why we tremble,
        want it more than anything.

The glint in her eyes
will be lost in the jaws
of a coyote that always starves.

Signs reading *Señorita Extraviada*
arrive daily at the dead-letter office.

For artistic purposes, the woman sits
on a spinning stool. Her eyes
like dull crystal beads
drag from left of camera, to camera, to right,
while she tries to sit straight
and regurgitate the names
dutifully   over and over.

Into the Dark Knots of Naked Walls

1
On a cold January night
the rusty bottom of a tin washtub
holds burning coals
until they turn to embers.

My father, with his articulate hands,
brings them inside the bare board walls,
lowers them in the middle
balanced on an upturned bucket
that totters over an earthen floor.
We position ourselves around it,
a brick block for each of us,
the radiance enough to make us
recognizable to each other.

This nucleus around which we hover
keeps us from drowning
into the dark knots of the naked walls,
the winter wind beating against them.

Sometimes the shins burn
and we must push away this anxious gravity
and when the distance threatens the cotton fibers
of the worn out denim shivering against our bodies,
we move back into the heat.

It goes on all evening,
this clumsy rocking of bodies
moving around the center
to keep from freezing –
slippery geography.

This is the lesson I can't forget.

2

In America,
the room we share is smaller,
too small to allow us all
a place around the gas heater
so we take turns sitting next to it
until we burn –
the ceramic bricks delicate
in their luminescence,
their dangerous generosity.

3

My eyelids warm over my eyes,
I hear the voice of a teacher
bald before a black board
speak of maps,
static in a color-by-numbers simplicity
and I see now he is wrong –
borders are dirt in a box,
rough, unsteady but holding everything living.
There is a constant motion,
a sad jockeying for position.

4

Between moves
I dream I pull away in the night
with the embers that I have stolen
from the center embedded in my chest,
my chest that becomes a bundle of maps
crumpled to keep me warm,
to cheat the shifting borders,
the tight folds of the hard paper
burning me and saving me
with every step I risk into the dark.

Meaning Enough for Peaches

The peaches in my aunt's backyard
whistle the same tune all afternoon –
the wind sifting thru the half-dry pit –
because the small animals without names
haven't come to pull them to pieces.

I think they know when I get home after school,
wait for me to come within hearing distance
to voice the dark recesses of their short lives.

Their taste comes to my ears, faint but piercing.

When I approach the longest branch,
the one on the edge of many edges,
the peaches begin to sway like bats
wincing their eyes away from the afternoon sun,
skin glowing a greenish yellow
that's just the right shade
to make you love them.

I hold a peach, motionless behind the leaves,
up to my eyes
until I marry it to my eyelid
and crush it between me and the thick branch,
my head clumsy with its own weight.

It is then that I see the pulp radiate violet,
bruised like all peaches must be
beneath their velvet coat,
perhaps no better than an obvious fig.

All of them bruises and velvet searching
to veil themselves behind the scant leaves.

Must everything that bruises be veiled?
Will everything veiled eventually bruise?

At school the science teacher spoke
about the meaning of life, how it wants
more than anything to be, and I wonder if,
in a world of gravitational fields and uneven orbits,
there is meaning enough for peaches.
Because they weep, they do,
hanging from a tree that I'm not supposed to touch,
grateful for the heft of my solitary stare.

And yet the foot bruises with every step
and sometimes people hug hard
and their faces begin to redden
but they don't let go.

My eye tastes the sweet lilac womb,
the juice flows down my right cheek,
mixing with a little blood from my brow
because here too my body learns to give.

And the leaves, spurred by the wind,
come to rustle in my ear that I must leave,
walk away while the peaches remain
dangling behind me.
I imagine that one day I pick them all
and rest them gently in a basket,
bruised and bruising each other.

The Little Rooms

I want to photograph the first house
I lived in when we came to this side.

My aunt still rents it out. The roof lower
of course, the walls thinner, brittle,
the crawl space still with shadow.

A room for a bed, a cot, and drawers,
a room with a breakfast table –
what I see is all there is,
the rest is the remnants of insects.

I'm certain that before
another school year ends,
the rooms will be condemned by the city –
perhaps they've always been – demolished
with a large hammer and one man's muscle.
Someone needing a meal.

I want to ask my aunt
*Can I take some photos
of the little rooms?* Like that, in those words
                                    – the little rooms.

But the image of me
with a $200 digital camera in my hand
before this that still meets my gaze
saddens me in indeterminate places.

The new family scraping
the same old linoleum inside
will pretend not to hear.
It will become easy to ignore them,
snap a few shots. I will want to walk inside,
but I won't ask them to let me.

My steps will be sure, cushioned by new shoes.
Convinced I have tricked or cheated something
like lessons learned without my parents' consent.

When I walk away my aunt will stand
behind her screen door. Her grandchildren
will pick their noses and stare at the shiny car I drive.

The camera will hold me in, contain
the homeless ghosts that I have stored
in the back rooms of newer homes,
the better homes, all the words I know
wringing their hands outside this
that is beautiful because it has splintered
the images in my eyes,
this that I want to remember
when I don't remember my own name.

1979 Chicago Avenue

This is the address on my grade school records,
the one I have to learn in case I ever get lost
or abducted by the man I never see
who rides slowly along neighborhood streets.

1979 – the shack where we first
exhale like wondering
if we've arrived, our jaws slack,
tongues almost saying: America,
the other side. Whatever we've carried
loosening itself from our hands.

Every night I lie in bed
between my parents.
The rest surrender on the floor
along with the rats and cockroaches
that after a while become familiar
with their curious antennae.

In lean dreams I swim across a river
and hope I don't drown tangled up
in the mossy mesquite branches
beneath the surface.

When the heat brings me back too soon,
when no other bodies stir,
like they've lost all will, I stumble out
through the hiss of the stove pilot,
the faded flowers of the floor,
the screen door's rusty latch
and bring my face to the floorboards outside.

The early morning mist
wets my limbs and as I drift back
into sleep, I whisper a prayer.

When I wake again in time for school,
my mother is lying next to me,
holding me close, and I know
this must be home.

Acknowledgments

Grateful acknowledgment is made to the editors and staff of the following publications where some of these poems, some in earlier versions, first appeared or are forthcoming:

580 Split: "Between Snores and Polyester"
Antenna: "Father" (formerly titled "Still")
Caduceus: "In a Yawn"
Connecticut Review: "Buick with Automatic Windows" and "Kraft American Cheese"
cream city review: "On watching a PBS documentary in the middle of the night"
The Fourth River: "Fuchsia" and "The Glass Always Almost Invisible"
Lips: "The Little Rooms"
The New York Quarterly: "Imagine a Tree"
Paterson Literary Review: "Veins like Maps," "Freshman Class Schedule," "The Confidence of Their Knees," "Joe, I never write about you" and "1979 Chicago Avenue" (formerly titled "2006 Chicago Avenue")
Ragazine.cc (online): "Blades of the Window Fan" and "Avocado"
The Red Clay Review: "Crushed Aspirin" and "Geometry" (formerly titled "Lázaro")
Rio Grande Review: "Whooping Cough (from my mother's memory)," (formerly titled "Whooping Cough")
The Spoon River Poetry Review: "Piñatas Too Small for Candy"

"Playing Monopoly" appears in the anthology *The American Voice in Poetry: The Legacy of Whitman, Williams, and Ginsberg,* edited by Maria Mazziotti Gillan

"Veins like Maps" won the 2009 Allen Ginsberg Poetry Award

I'd like to thank the communities at UT - Pan American and SUNY-Binghamton for welcoming me.

Many thanks to all who read parts/versions of this in manuscript form and offered insight and encouragement. Much gratitude to Maria Mazziotti Gillan, Joe Weil, and Leslie Heywood for their generosity, support, and guidance. Thank you to Emmy Pérez, René Saldaña, Jr., Melinda Mejia, Sarah Jefferis, Kristi M. Costello, and Kim Vose.

A whole bunch of thank you's to Luis J. Rodríguez and Tía Chucha Press for believing in this work. Me llena de emoción.

Always grateful to my family for their love through all my incarnations. *Mil gracias a mi madre y a mi padre, los quiero y los llevo conmigo siempre.*

To the grade-school teachers of my childhood who showed me kindness – I carry it with me.